WHY YOUR MARKETING
IS KILLING YOUR BUSINESS

And what to do about it

Here to you! for all you do! I hope this book makes you smile! To your success!

By Minal Sampat

Ordering Information: Quantity sales. Special discounts are available on quantity purchases by corporations, associations, and others. For details, contact the publisher at the address above.

This book is dedicated to the clients and colleagues who have allowed me to be a part of their business journey. While most names have been changed, your stories and experiences made this book possible. Thank you for trusting me and your unwavering support.

To your success,
Minal Sampat

Contents

The Marketing Illusion

Every day I talk to clients looking for a quick marketing fix, the latest tactic or service that will help them find more customers than they can handle. That vision is an illusion. There's no one simple trick to becoming an overnight success. If there was, we'd be sitting on yachts reading a very different book than this one.

Ask any successful business owner you know how they got where they are, and the word *overnight* probably won't appear in the answer. There is, however, something that can be maintained and renewed over time that gets consistent results. To illustrate, let me share something from my time growing up in India.

When I was five years old, I lived in a house that had a beautiful hand-carved wooden porch swing. Everyone loved the swing and took turns sitting on it to enjoy the sunshine, breeze, and passing of the day.

Every afternoon my uncle, Dr. Narendra Sampat and I would sit on the swing and he would tell me stories. This was my favorite part of the day: learning about the past, living in the present, and dreaming about the future. These stories connected me to his childhood, travels, music, happenings in his practice, and life experiences.

If you think about it, connection is all around us. Online and offline, we're members of social and professional networks. We use smartphones and even smart homes and cars. Like us, our customers have more information available to them, and can act on it more quickly than ever before. However, despite all of this increased communication, information, and marketing, it is somehow harder to make a connection that converts.

If your marketing efforts don't focus on overcoming this competitive noise, your business will fail to connect. In the marketing industry, this is known as Shiny Object Syndrome, when every business is so busy screaming for attention, using the newest tools, and highlighting their best qualities that the noise is deafening, the highlights blinding. It's hard to pick any single business out of the crowd.

That is what marketing looks like today. Promotional tactics are hawked by companies as quick and easy, but quick and easy doesn't get results. Today's consumers are too smart; marketing doesn't give them enough credit. They can see right past the facade. This is why I say your marketing is killing your business.

What customers today crave is something real. They want to feel something rather than be pitched to. They want to connect.

The chase to find the new, hot marketing magic bullet is misguided advice. At best, it is a marketing miscalculation. It just doesn't add up in today's over-stimulated world. The better strategy is not to be different, but to find common ground to connect on.

Connection is key. I say this because it works. Over the years, it has worked again and again for my clients and attendees. It's what made me fall in love with marketing, what got me my first job, what drove me to open a company, and what helped me see how badly we need to shift our marketing mindset. A shift in our approach as business owners is necessary to stay competitive.

With this book, I hope to show you how to focus on connection and let go of the illusion of a secret marketing weapon. It's time to stop pretending and get real. It's time to connect with people.

Switch From Promotion To Connection

With whom is your business trying to connect? You may be tempted to say *everyone*, but that isn't true. In fact, that's how the current white noise problem started in the first place.

At minimum, you are looking for customers, clients, or patients who can afford your products or services. Not only that, you also want to connect with people who will benefit from what you offer, with bonus points if they already know they'll benefit, and are seeking you out.

Let's go even deeper.

Who Is Your Who?

Take a moment to think about someone you feel close to, perhaps a friend, family member, or significant other. Odds are, if I asked you about their likes, dislikes, frustrations, needs, and wants, you'd be able to list them fairly easily.

Can you do the same for your customers? While you don't have to become best friends with your customers (or marry them, for that matter), it's important to be aware of the tastes and needs of your business's ideal demographics.

Where do they live, work, shop, and travel? What technologies do they use? How do they make purchasing decisions? All of this information is important in creating your **ideal customer avatar**, which is a picture of the person with whom you are trying to connect. Once you know who you are trying to reach, directing resources towards connecting with them becomes that much easier.

Reaching five hundred residents near your business's geographic area can be accomplished with many different marketing tools. However, without an accurate customer avatar, there's a cold audience receiving a broad, white noise message from your business. You don't just want brand exposure; you want conversions.

Today's consumers require connection and casting a wide net rarely does the trick. In the past, a general campaign might reach thousands of people and generate a hundred leads. Today, campaigns need to identify those one hundred perfect customers first and focus on targeting them specifically. Deep, meaningful connection is formed when efforts are focused on the few people who match your customer avatar.

By streamlining your efforts in this way, a more meaningful message is received by a warmer audience. How? Let's use an example to illustrate.

Your service-based business wants to attract young families. Putting up flyers and buying newspaper ads isn't going to reach the majority of that audience because they're young professionals with children. Convenience and quality are of utmost importance to this demographic. The questions you need to ask yourself are:

1. Are you easy to find on search engines, digital and social media platforms, and family groups/blogs?

2. What are other people saying about you in online reviews, township/parent groups, and via word of mouth?

3. How convenient is it to schedule with you by phone and online?

4. Are your wait time and customer service up to par?

5. Is your business space family- and children-friendly?

If, for another example, we decide to shift away from young families and look at the golden generation, we have to change tactics. As seniors, many of them require less technology, more empathy, and plenty of patience. The approach is completely different.

In order to effectively connect with your audience, you need to know who your ideal audience is and how to meet them where they are. You can break through the marketing white noise by zeroing in on exactly what your customers want and need, and explain how you provide exactly that.

Many marketing approaches attempt to reach consumers on a broad scale. The attempt fails if the message is too general, trying to reach too many people. Once you have identified your ideal customer avatar, you know who you are reaching out to. It's this that informs your decision on how to connect.

Here are **Five Ways To Connect** that get results:

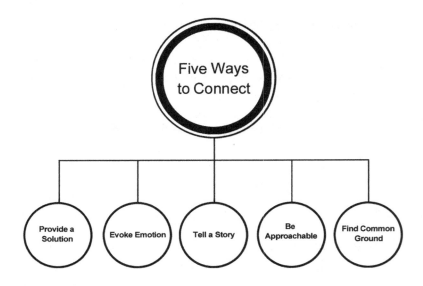

Provide A Solution

One of the most common ways businesses connect with customers is by providing a solution to a problem. Whether offering necessary services such as dental care, tax advice, or increasing quality of life for customers by selling the equivalent of a cold smoothie on a hot day, customers will connect with businesses who acknowledge their problem and solve it.

Some customers need solutions at a certain time, such as after they get off work at 5:00 p.m. Adding before- and after-work hours, and/or weekend hours, meets those customers' needs. By providing services at that time, you solve a problem.

Another way to provide a solution is by answering questions. For example, a weekly Q&A hosted on social media or your website establishes you as an authority and solution provider in your industry. Facebook Live video is a great tool to use for this and also encourages viewers to follow your Facebook page. This Q&A allows you to connect with people who have questions related to the services or products you provide and offers an opportunity for them to see you authentically.

This doesn't just have to happen online. Q&A sessions at the end of speaking engagements are often more engaging and exciting than the actual talk itself. In these forums, you meet people with real problems and have the opportunity to provide direct solutions to those problems, forging true connections.

When we are solution-oriented, our business is no longer about us, but about our customers. We move away from being self-focused on *my* talk, *my* topic, *my* services, *my* products, or *my* whatever. Instead, we stop and say, Wait, what do *they* need? How can I help my customers, clients, or patients?

Evoke Emotion

One much-discussed athletic wear commercial highlighted the conception of female athletes as "crazy", playing clips of competitors reacting passionately to wins, losses, bad calls, and more at sporting events.

For the audience, watching these expressions compiled back-to-back makes it hard not to react emotionally. The athletic wear company knows this and used it to their advantage.

Customers have a way of remembering how a brand makes them feel. Make them feel impassioned, and that impression of the brand will last.

Emotion is a huge part of sales. People buy with emotion. Major brands often tug at heartstrings, completely ignoring the quality of their products, simply to strike an emotional chord and win business. Take soda companies, for example. If they shared their ingredients in their marketing, people would likely stop buying soda.

Instead, soda companies encourage you to share the sweet drink with a friend, displaying images of people laughing and enjoying themselves with the product. This has nothing to do with the quality of the product, and everything to do with the emotions associated with having fun and belonging.

Medication commercials do this as well, slipping side effects in as quickly and quietly as legally allowed while showing images of people enjoying the outdoors and spending time with loved ones.

While this tactic has a long history in marketing, the best methods today for businesses are the ones which involve identifying what your niche audience wants. After that, it's all about showing how your business provides that in a way that *feels* good.

Your business can also harness the power of emotion to connect with your existing customers. Photos and videos of happy customers smiling and captions with quotes about how your product or service impacted them, go a long way.

Tell A Story

Telling a story is an intentional sharing of your life and experiences. It doesn't have to evoke strong emotions, though it can. When you open yourself up to others, you connect naturally with people because you are sharing your life with them.

When you tell a story, instead of customers seeing you as a business, they connect with you as a person. They value you differently. I know this because I recently saw the phenomenon firsthand.

I made a video about how I was traveling through an airport and wound up out of breath after having to run to my gate. I realized I need to show up for myself more and get in shape. By sharing this personal struggle and desire to get healthier, I started a journey with my audience.

When I shared that story, I got an amazing amount of feedback. People were inspired to take their own health seriously, and I even had press reach out to share my journey on their publications. I was honest about my experience, even the difficult parts, including that I hired a personal trainer because I knew it was the only way I would stick to my goal. That sincerity mattered to my listeners.

How did I relate this to marketing? I asked my audience to take a look at their goals, at what they wanted to achieve. I encouraged them to find roadblocks and solutions to them. I did this in my personal life, I explained, and you can do it in your marketing.

As a business owner who wants returning customers, you want your audience to feel that they are a part of your journey, and you a part of theirs. Picture a brewer selling his beer at a weekly farmer's market. He brews this beer in his backyard and shares his story with first-time customers. Customers feel like they are a part of his business's journey, which is also his personal journey. His story turns them into returning customers. The beer is tasty, but it isn't all that brings customers back week after week: it's the brewer and his story.

Sharing a part of your journey makes you more human. It takes away the formality of business, giving it a human face.

Be Approachable

Your customers' perception of you is important to connection. Regardless of what stories you share or problems you solve, connecting by being kind, personable, and genuine with customers is a long-lasting way to maintain a good impression.

Think of the last great restaurant server you had, someone who knew the dishes, made good recommendations and had a great attitude and smile. Even if the food was just okay, you remember this server because of how easy it was to connect with them. Similarly, if you reflect on a time you received terrible service, the quality of food likely didn't really matter if the service tainted the experience. Apply that knowledge to your business.

If you're walking down the street, and you make eye contact with a stranger who kindly smiles and waves, you're likely to return the gesture. That's a connection. It comes to us naturally.

This connection is key to marketing. With content, for example, you want material that is approachable, not too formal, too heavy, or hard to read. Approachable photos on social media and your website are similarly important.

This also applies to customer service. If you run a hotel, you want your front desk person to be willing to help, even going out of their way, to provide a pleasant experience and service. This results in good reviews and returning customers, and is as easy as being genuine and down-to-earth in your concern for your customers' experience.

Many business owners and public figures now have online video shows. A video show is an accessible platform that allows viewers to directly connect and share their questions and concerns. It's an easy way to put your best foot forward to a larger audience.

Is being on camera not your thing? You can still show that you're available to chat in other ways. For example, you can open your #TipTuesday social media post up to questions. *What do you think of this tip? Will you use it? How could we use it better?* You can have an ideas box at your storefront or schedule a time to meet your customers on a daily or weekly basis.

Being approachable means giving someone a safe space to ask questions, make requests, and utilize the outlet to connect. The key is ease of communication. Your business should be like the people wearing *Ask Me* shirts at large events: easy to spot in a crowd, and permission to approach clearly given.

Find Common Ground

In a time where differentiation is the trend, I ask you to find common ground. This often means opening up a bit, revealing experiences others may relate to, or sharing something as simple as, for example, your passion for shoes.

When my husband and I moved into our first place together, we had to convert the second bedroom into a closet for all my shoes. While humorous, my love for shoes has actually connected me to a number of clients who also love shoes, even though shoes have nothing to do with marketing or business. To my delight and surprise, I've even received shoes from clients as a thank you gift!

Sharing personal, relatable passions is one way to find common ground, but if it's not your style, it's not required.

If you have been working in your industry for a while, you know the ins and outs, and the lingo. Use that knowledge. A dental hygienist breaking into consulting, for example, has experience working with dental patients. They know the systems used in dental offices, how the day's pace increases and slows, and have been through the experience of scheduling and handling patient concerns. This knowledge can be used to connect with dental practitioners in need of a consultant. It demonstrates the ability to meet practitioners where they are.

What do you have in common with the people in your industry? What familiar language do you speak, and how can you meet them where they are coming from?

Remember my afternoons on the porch swing, listening to stories from my uncle? What do you feel as I bring that memory back to your attention? Making a connection is as easy as that. Even when you are trying to sell, finding common ground will connect you, and your business, with people.

We are more alike than we are different. Focus on similarities, rather than the differences, and you'll find success.

Quality, Not Quantity

Amanda ran a small, tight-knit healthcare practice out of a cozy location in Midwestern America. With just two providers and a need to expand their patient base, Amanda decided to engineer a promotional discount to bring in new patients. It worked! The promotion increased the practice's new patient numbers from 35 a month to 42.

It was a noteworthy accomplishment, but the celebration was short-lived. Despite reaching and treating more patients, the practice's production remained stagnant over time. They were accommodating more patients and not seeing a reflection of it in revenue, and Amanda couldn't figure out why. It was time to reach out for help.

When I took a look at Amanda's marketing, the problem became clear: the new promotion was bringing in patients, but they weren't the kind of patients who would stick around. Known as deal shoppers, these new patients were bargain-hunters, coming in for the advertised first-visit reduced price with no intention of returning.

"You are going to have to stop running that promotion," I told Amanda.

"The new promotion is the only reason we've seen an increase in new patients," she worried. "Without it, how can there be any guarantee that we won't start losing revenue?"

"It's a risk you'll have to take to gain long-term stability," I explained. The current method simply wasn't working.

After putting in time to identify a better target audience and where to find them, the old promotion was pulled, and new marketing went out to attract leads more likely to become lifelong patients.

It was scary at first, but not long after, production was up by 20%. What's more, this increased production was up even while the number of new patients slightly dropped. The new target audience had more patients looking for a long-term relationship with their healthcare provider, not a bargain.

Business owners could learn a lot from these new patients who sought out quality connections, rather than focusing on the numbers.

The story above is not uncommon. Many businesses fall into Amanda's trap, obsessing over the quantity of new customers rather than the quality of their lifetime value. The problem isn't necessarily the promotional discount tactic, since many business models benefit greatly from drawing in bargain shoppers. The important thing is to figure out whether bargain shoppers are your business's ideal target audience, and whether that connection is worth it.

The Right Message For The Right Audience

By focusing on getting your messaging in front of the right audience, your business can better attract best-fit customers.

This focus on quality applies to your marketing budget as well. Businesses will spend a lot on TV ads, billboards, newspapers, church bulletins, websites, social media, and beyond. They focus on putting out high-quantity marketing on as many platforms as possible. This isn't necessarily effective.

Instead, businesses really just need to focus on two things:

1. The target audience

2. What services or products attracts them

No matter how you are trying to grow your business, every strategy starts by looking at your business model. Knowing who your bread-and-butter customers are, whether returners or one-time purchasers, informs you about the audience you want and what attracts them.

Once you know your target audience and what to sell, you can start shifting your messaging to marketing outlets that work to meet those goals. I've seen businesses reduce marketing budgets by twenty percent or more to see not only revenue retained, but also more customers coming in thanks to targeted marketing on platforms chosen with intention.

One way businesses explore their target audience is by coming up with their ideal customer avatar. This isn't a new idea I can take credit for. It's a well-known and highly effective practice in the marketing world.

Your ideal customer avatar is a customer profile that is a best-case scenario for your business. Perhaps it's someone who is a big spender, a regular who consistently returns, someone who speaks well of your business in their networks, or all three.

There are two ways to discover your ideal customer avatar. If you have already been in business for a few years, you may have read the description above and realized you already know your ideal customer avatar because they're an actual customer of yours!

If that's the case, ask yourself, *What do I like about this person?* It might be their timeliness, their connection to the community around your business, their willingness to pay prices as quoted, or something else. These valuable qualities of your superhero customer are the ones you want to seek out in your target audience.

By focusing on the favorable characteristics of your best customer, you can start seeking out new quality customers like them rather than expending energy and money raking in quantity.

A Vision Of Your Ideal Customer

If you don't already have an ideal customer, you'll need to come up with a vision for one on your own. This is an exercise I do often with clients and meeting attendees alike, and it's quite easy. You can do it right now.

Take a moment to think about your business, and who you would really love to see walking in the door. What is this customer's:

- Age?
- Gender?
- Profession?
- Social circle?
- Hobbies?

- Income?
- Work & home locations?
- Relationship status?

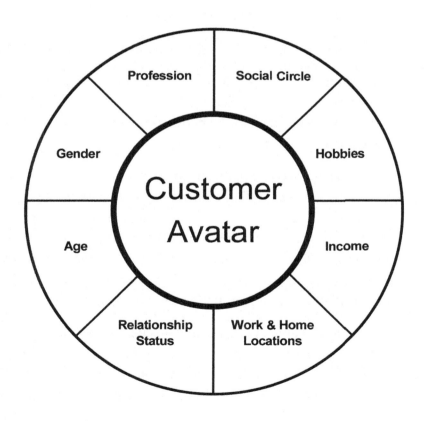

Next, ask yourself:

- Does this customer have children?

- How did they get to my door?

- Do they live in the area, or are they visiting/seasonal?

- How far do they live/work from my business?

- Where do they spend their free time?

- Are they looking for a bargain, or for the best quality?

- Do they travel? Date? Enjoy happy hours?

- Where do they turn for recommendations, and how?

As an example, let's say I own a fitness gym, and I'd really like to attract more middle-class mothers who I know live in my area because I often see them dropping their children off at the daycare across the street.

My ideal customer in this situation is likely aged twenty-five to forty, in the professional field, married, living and working within ten miles, making average to above-average income. She likely socializes with other mothers, possibly enjoys brunch, book clubs, taking her kids to the park, wine tastings, and occasional travel. She'll pay for nice things but is practical with her budget. Perhaps her name is Morgan.

You may laugh at me giving her a name, but this is actually a very important part of the avatar creation process. Giving your ideal customer a name makes them more real, more relatable, and more easily envisioned walking through your door.

So, what is your avatar's name? Go on and pick one, if you haven't already.

Once you have an avatar named and envisioned, it becomes exponentially easier to target your messaging to that person. This is a really powerful exercise. I've led workshops around avatar development for owners of businesses of all industries and sizes, all marketing budgets, at various locations, and all of them benefited from naming their avatar. All walked out of the meeting or workshop with a marketing plan in hand.

Once you know this avatar really well, you'll know what to offer them to get them in your door.

If I'm a fitness gym owner trying to attract Morgan, I may need to offer Mommy & Me classes at the gym, or even at the daycare across the street. Perhaps I could advertise by creating and sharing healthy family meal plans, or even reach out to the local farmers' market and juice bars for opportunities to collaborate and cross-market.

In terms of the internet, where is Morgan online? Based on her age, she likely uses Facebook and Instagram. That's where I'll spend my budget, not on Snapchat or a newspaper ad and not anywhere Morgan won't be. Healthy family meal plans, if I decide to use them, can be shared on the platforms where Morgan already spends her time.

What if one day, Morgan decides she wants to start working out on her own, before even seeing any of my messaging? How will she look for my business?

She'll probably want a gym close to home. She may prioritize a gym that provides childcare and/or play areas. What makes my gym the best choice for mothers like Morgan in our neighborhood? Do I have parent meet and greets, or encourage playdates? Are there ways my gym encourages members to meet workout partners to stay motivated?

The idea is, now that I know that I'm trying to attract Morgan, I can better direct my messaging and budget towards that effort, rather than taking guesses. I can raise my chances of connecting with my ideal customer instead of overwhelming multiple platforms with directionless messaging just hoping I'll catch someone's eye among all the white noise.

You don't have to use every platform available to share your message, in turn becoming another shiny object. You just have to connect with the actual people you want in your business.

You don't have to spend hundreds of thousands of dollars on, for example, funnels. That's not to say that anything is wrong with funnels. No platform is wrong, just as with the promotional discount I shared earlier. There are simply so many options that you need to figure out which ones to focus on for your business's model, target audience, and message. You need to figure out how to make a connection among all the options available.

How are your customers finding you? If you're a small business in a small town, you'll want to market at small local events. Throwing money at Google may not be the most efficient use of each dollar. Location is just as important as the individual's demographics.

You want to make things easy for people. If you make it easy for Morgan to choose you, she will.

Millennials like myself grew up with technology and we can be busy running businesses, traveling, and balancing multiple roles. As a result, I will consistently choose to schedule or chat online, text, and send emails rather than pick up the phone. If you're trying to attract the young, tech-savvy crowd, spend your money on those tools. However, if you are trying to attract my father, a baby boomer, your spending will be focused elsewhere. You'll likely need a fantastic, friendly, and patient team member to call him on the phone or meet in person to talk. It's all about what your target market prefers.

Your budget should be tailored to your target audience. This isn't a numbers game; it's about quality. Once you know your target market and are spending money to get in front of them, the job's not over yet. It's important to figure out your ROI. Where are your conversions coming from? Where is the spending justified?

Maximize your best messaging avenues. Out of the ten you're using, which five are really working? Get rid of the least effective ones, narrow down where your best results are coming from, and focus your money there. This will prevent you from throwing away marketing dollars that see little return for the effort.

Really understanding what is working is important. Effective marketing isn't set-it-and-forget-it. It's a constantly evolving endeavor as your business and target audience, as well as platforms available to connect with them, change over time.

True connection is an ongoing relationship with your customer avatar and your business. Nurture it like any other relationship and you'll see results.

Leverage, Not Follow

When I start working with a client for the first time, I often begin with a question: What are you already doing for marketing?

One of my clients, John, offered a common answer: Everything!

John had been running a family business with his wife in the same neighborhood for over thirty years. They were both baby boomers, hardworking and versatile even in the toughest times. The business had a great reputation and was well-known and loved by the community, but growth had plateaued. They needed to reignite things to keep the business healthy.

Trying to stay competitive with others in the industry, John reached out to a website development and maintenance company in his professional network. He paid approximately $15,000 for a new site and content and signed up for search engine optimization (SEO) services. This was in addition to the existing marketing he'd already been doing for decades. It really felt like he was trying everything, and yet, the business didn't see any growth in revenue. Without growth, it would be impossible to continue to improve the business

27

and keep services and products up to date. John needed a solution.

I understood his need as soon as he reached out to me, as well as his frustration at having tried everything. I agreed to take a look at his marketing efforts and offer some insight.

When I evaluated the marketing expenditure, three major issues were revealed:

1. *Some of the marketing outlets already in place were not being maximized, creating missed opportunities.*

2. *A few service providers, like the website company, were not producing results. In fact, they couldn't even produce SEO reports.*

3. *Much of the marketing was done just because it was popular at the time, with no strategy or follow-up.*

I secured a refund for the SEO services, but John was understandably discouraged. He'd been working with these companies for quite some time and had built a relationship with them. He thought the companies would provide the best services for his business without him having to follow-up. They'd breached his trust, and he felt overwhelmed and confused.

Once we created a cohesive marketing plan specific to his target market and filled in missing gaps with the right tools and resources, things became easier. In nine months, John learned how to streamline and leverage his marketing efforts. He and I were able to reduce his marketing budget by $20,000 by removing unnecessary expenditure and ignoring *marketing fads. We reallocated the remainder to increase his revenue and get the business back on a growth track.*

John thought he was leveraging his marketing budget to maximum effect. He was doing what the other professionals in his network were doing. As it turned out, however, following the crowd on this decision cost him a lot of money, time, and stress.

Resist Marketing Peer Pressure

This reaffirms a really important lesson in our current communication landscape: just because everyone is doing it, doesn't mean you have to. There's no need to add to the white noise if you're not sure it'll be right for your business. Doing the trendy thing without attempting to connect with ideal customers, or avatars, contributes to the Shiny Object Syndrome. This applies even if what your competitors are doing works for them.

Once we have identified our own target audience and message, regardless of what competitors are doing, we can more accurately determine what the best medium for reaching those people with that message is. It may be a website, specific social media channel, reputation site, a billboard, a TV ad, or something else.

Now, I'm not going to tell you *not* to diversify your mediums to gain a wider audience. What I will say, however, is once you've chosen a medium that is right for your audience and message, you need to do everything you can to maximize the use of that medium.

If you're doing a TV commercial, for example, and can only provide an amateurly filmed video, the commercial company will likely simply air the video as provided. That's a waste of your money. Imagine seeing shaky camera footage and straining to hear weak audio during a football watch party. No one will take that business seriously, and that commercial will not be leveraged or maximized. It's not engaging, is poorly made, and won't attract your potential customers.

Every opportunity to connect has its own similar considerations:

Print mailers. You know mailers end up in someone's hand, and you want it to stay there rather than get tossed with the junk. According to one neuroscience study by Canada Post[1], direct mail is more memorable and more persuasive than digital media but is visually processed quicker. Because of this, it needs to be relevant to the recipient, eye-catching, perhaps even funny, to stand out among the rest of the mail.

Radio commercials. For radio ads, you need to know which audiences are listening to which stations and target the stations where your audience demographics match those of listeners. Jingles help, obviously. I'm sure you still remember some radio or TV jingles from your own childhood.

Billboards. Billboards reach a lot of viewers but can still be strategically placed geographically. They also require

---

[1]   "A Bias for Action: The neuroscience behind the response-driving power of direct mail," Canada Post, July 31, 2015, https://www.canadapost.ca/assets/pdf/blogs/CPC_Neuroscience_EN_150717.pdf.

eye-catching layouts for drivers who are speeding by. Too much writing will get ignored given the short exposure time. Quick, clear, and engaging is key, such as an easy-to-remember website URL or phone number, for example.

Social media. Currently, Facebook's most productive content is Live videos. To best leverage Live videos, you need to announce when you'll be live so people can anticipate it. You can decide to go live at a time based on Facebook's analytics showing you when most of your fans are online. You can also stay live for at least ten minutes to give fans plenty of time to join you. Once they're there, say hello on camera, welcome them to the experience, and connect.

I'm often asked, *Will something go wrong?* The answer is, *Everything that can go wrong, will go wrong with your first Live.* Don't despair. Just be your authentic self and react with humor. Your viewers will continue to connect with you. Live video success is not determined by the situation, but by how you react to it.

That is how you maximize Facebook today. Instagram is different. You'll need to learn how to correctly use hashtags and use the right kind. Your content will be focused on visual storytelling and maximizing Instagram stories.

Leverage your messaging by not just doing what everyone else does, instead doing what makes sense for your business and your audience. Not everyone needs to be on all social media platforms. You just need to be on the platforms where your target audience is.

Making The Most Of Connections

Whatever platforms you're on, leverage them as much as possible. As I said earlier, connection is not a set-it-and-forget-it solution. It is a tool you must consistently use to tweak your messaging to meet evolving market needs.

This all may sound like a lot, and that's because it is. It's why people like me exist, to sort through the fluff marketing that is killing your business and to hone in on what's right for you.

Service providers in particular talk a big game when it comes to converting leads to customers. How do you cut through the white noise and figure out who you can trust?

The answer is to have some knowledge about how things work. It's okay to pay experts to do the things you aren't sure how to do yourself. It's smart, even! You don't know what you don't know, but not knowing anything about how a service is provided makes it hard to know whether you're getting your money's worth. Having just some knowledge will help you identify who you can trust.

Here are some questions I encourage you to ask the next time you're talking with someone offering marketing services:

1. What specific services do you offer?

2. How are you going to provide those services?

3. How are you going to communicate with me? (How will I know your service is producing results? Will

I hear from you monthly, biweekly? Via reports, meetings, or updates?)

4. What results should I expect, and by when, once I start working with you?

5. Can you provide recent industry and client references who aren't referral affiliates?

If the company doesn't have an answer for these questions, then they're probably not meeting the full spectrum of basic needs for reliable service delivery.

Imagine, for example, a company calls you offering to put up a billboard for your business. You might ask whether you'll design the billboard, or the company? If the company designs it, do you get a say in the design? How many times can you request a redesign? Do they have some samples of previous work you can see? Have they done a billboard for your industry before? What were the results?

If a service provider can't answer similar questions, they may not be prepared to provide quality service. Providers should be able to tell you what they do. You need this information to plan your business's marketing strategy, and they need to provide this information to build trust.

Once you've gotten answers, go online and research the company. Read their reviews. Find their social media pages and inspect their business culture. If another professional has recommended a company to you, ask them if they receive referral fees or any kind of monies from that company.

Then, and this is important: wait. There's no need to rush. Go through these checks, take time to think about their answers, come up with follow-up questions, and wait to hear back from references, especially if you are buying into a big service.

Innovation is great. It's new, exciting, and different. The issue, however, is that not every innovation is right for you.

For example, a client of mine wanted to improve their online reviews, but most of their clientele were not tech-savvy, and many didn't have Facebook, Yelp, or Google accounts, let alone the knowledge to use their review systems.

Online reviews are very important to businesses today, so if your current clientele can't provide them, it's easy to feel stuck. As their marketing strategist, I worked together with the client to overcome this hurdle. We tried everything to get more reviews, even creating how-to pamphlets on how to create email accounts step-by-step. At first, nothing seemed to work, but it was my job to keep working to figure it out.

They had happy customers who really wanted to help, but simply didn't have the technological literacy to do so. How could we leverage that? We needed another approach. I suggested that we start asking customers if they'd be comfortable writing a handwritten note or making a quick video.

Instead of having them post online, we took photos of customers and their handwritten reviews, using the photos and a typed version of the notes as content for social media, online platforms, and Google posts. We then boosted this content so that more people would see it, since it wasn't appearing naturally in reviews.

More typical review platforms were working for the competition, but they weren't working for this client. We had to figure out what would. As we moved forward, we used the business's email system to see which customers already had Gmail addresses, and only sent them requests specifically for Google reviews. We knew they wouldn't have to create a Google account since they already had one.

We did the same thing for Facebook, only asking customers who became followers or checked in on the social media platform to leave Facebook reviews. With these two new approaches combined, online reviews, both in review platforms and in our boosted post format, started rolling in— and so did new customers.

If something doesn't work for your business, but you still need it, figure out how to leverage what you have. Use what's going to work for you, either because you already have it, or because you've identified your target market and message and the conclusion you've reached makes sense. Solve problems in ways that are most useful to you.

Don't just follow what's happening with others. Leverage your platforms, your products, your systems, and your team. Build solutions with your target audience and message in mind to maximize those existing resources and make the most of your budget. Create a cohesive plan for each marketing outlet in your customer's buying journey to avoid dropout along the way.

Here's a simplified visualization of a customer's journey:

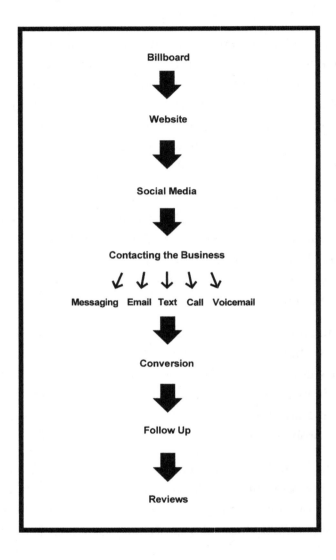

When you connect the dots and personalize systems to your needs, you start to leverage and not follow.

Teamwork, Not Micromanagement

Dr. Brunsden and Dr. Villa have been in business since 1985. They are the proud owners of KidZdent, a pediatric and orthodontic practice with a strong concentration on serving the autistic community. With the help of over forty team members, their practice has served multiple generations of patients, earning them recognition as leaders in their field.

When Drs. Brunsden and Villa went into business in the 1980s, marketing was very different. By 2008, as Facebook gained momentum, they knew what social media was but didn't have the tools to leverage it. Their relationship with the community was strong, but as savvy and successful business owners they understood the importance of utilizing social media to stay ahead of the curve.

After my internship at KidZdent as a Rutgers student, the doctors took me onto the team. They weren't sure what title to give me, or exactly what tasks to assign, but they trusted that my ambition, youth, and experience with the practice as an intern would result in good things.

They were right, and in some unexpected ways. I not only wanted to build the practice's first-ever social media account, but also create online business listings. This would open up the practice to online reviews visible to the world with little control over what was being said. Drs. Brunsden and Villa had a great offline reputation. Would it be the same online?

"It's like going from 'word of mouth' to 'world of media'," Dr. Brunsden joked.*

I knew that despite the hesitancy, change had to happen. Social media and online reputation were not just a trend; they were the new reality. They were also right in my wheelhouse as a millennial who'd grown up with social media and online shopping. Most importantly, I knew that the risk of giving up some control over reviews was outweighed by the benefits. Patients loved Drs. Brunsden and Villa, and that would inevitably shine through online.

I believed in the practice and wanted the world to see it through my eyes. I knew that social media platforms would be the way to show off its great culture, both in how patients and the team were celebrated. I set to work creating online directories on sites such as Google and Healthgrades, updating the practice's website, finding a company to manage SEO, and building a Facebook page. Offline, I also began creating engagement with team members and patients in the office through team building and appreciation events.

This fun culture had many benefits. Happy team members gave great customer service, which meant happy customers who were likely to return, recommend friends, and, you guessed it, write great online reviews. Appreciation events like ice cream parties and team-building games also provided photo and video opportunities for the kind of content that gets social media users engaged. Just like today, the practice's audience wanted to connect and see the business as not just a service, but as a group of people who enjoyed what they were doing.

Over time, Drs. Brunsden and Villa's online presence became one of their top referral sources, boasting thousands of followers and reviews. They now have multiple active social media accounts in addition to Facebook. All of this is because they gave a recent college graduate with a passion for marketing the freedom and support to pursue those passions.

Drs. Brunsden and Villa are my mentors, and I'm grateful to them for the opportunity to explore my interests and discover my strengths. Through my experience with them, I learned that the best way business owners can get their team on board with growth is to include each team member's interests and strengths in the growth plan. Let people do what they enjoy doing, and you'll soon see their best work.

As a business owner, you can do anything, just not everything. That's what I tell my clients because, for most of them, it is physically impossible to run their business alone. You need a team, and teams are best when they work together to share their strengths.

Even my own business is an example of this. I may look like Wonder Woman managing to juggle speaking events, coaching, podcasting, masterminding, Live videoing, blogging, social mediaing (yes, that's a word), and book writing, but I actually have a team that I couldn't do it all without. Multiple assistants, writers, digital and social media managers, and even coaches of my own all contribute to my success. I've chosen each of those team members based on their strengths and passion for what I'm asking them to do.

The connection I have with my team members, and the one you should share with yours, is the foundation of the connection we create with our customers. If we can't even connect with the people working within our business, how can we hope to connect with those outside of it? Once we build our businesses on the practice of acknowledging people as individuals with unique personalities and interests, that belief will shine through in our messaging to outside audiences.

How do you accomplish this in your marketing? It takes a special team member.

Leveraging Your Team For Marketing

Tackling marketing in-house may seem daunting, but it doesn't have to be. If you're willing to give it a try, I guarantee it'll be more effective than having an outsider attempt to perfect your message and target audience. Whether you train someone already on your team, or bring on a new hire or intern, a dedicated marketing person can research and execute the best plans for your business and communicate with a strategist like me along the way.

With the right training, this person becomes your in-house marketing guru. All it takes is a genuine interest in connecting your business to its target audience. Over time, that dedicated team member, too, will understand the importance of connection over marketing and make your outreach worries obsolete.

Once you have selected or hired someone, this person will be monitoring new customers, acquisition cost, marketing ROI, internal marketing for current customers, and, here's the secret, they will also be working on building a happy team culture inside the business.

If that sounds like a lot of work, that's because it is. It takes work to run great campaigns as well as time, resources, and clear goals.

What this means is, first, **give this person time to do it all.** Simply assigning someone with an interest in marketing isn't enough if they're having to do it all on top of other work. They may need additional hours, a reduced workload in other areas, or even a part-time assistant. Don't overfill their glass and expect good results.

Next, **provide your specialist with clear goals**. What do you want to accomplish? What is your vision? With a quantifiable, measurable outcome in mind, your team member has a concrete target to aim for and can direct their efforts accordingly.

In addition to time and clear goals, **supply your dedicated team member with the resources necessary to complete the work they thrive at**. If they have a knack for making beautiful raffle baskets and want to use that skill to help your business, how can you ensure that they are easily able to get their hands on all the materials they need? This applies to whatever talents may be utilized to encourage connection within and outside of the business.

Every one of your team members has a unique talent. Give them a seat at the table to show off and talk about those talents, and watch it feed into your business's success.

Lastly, remember to be kind, and show appreciation for team members' work, especially when they've shared a personal part of themselves to contribute to your business growth. The most common negative feedback I hear from team members around the world is that they don't feel appreciated by their employers. Saying *thank you* is critical to maintaining good relationships long-term and keeping teams invested in a business's success.

Be authentic and respectful, using *please* when asking for something and *sorry* when a mistake is made. Being genuine builds positive connections within your team, so that they can build those connections with your customers.

When you create a safe workplace for people to share their talents, and thank them for doing so, you create a stronger team capable of taking on whatever changes the market throws their way. A team that knows and honors one another's strengths and weaknesses is the strongest working unit in business. Let people do what they enjoy, support others around them doing the same and see the results yourself.

A Word Of Caution

It can be tempting, of course, to want to exert some control over all of this free-flying passion. As business owners, we like guarantees and knowing that we're not wasting time, energy, or money.

While I certainly understand the concern, there is something I have to warn you against: micromanagement. Micromanagement is the death of creativity, and it absolutely will kill your most promising campaign ideas before they've even had a chance to fully form.

Talented people with good ideas need space, freedom, and time to show off their gifts. Here's how you can make sure that happens in your business:

Set a timeline for idea development. Give your team member(s) a project, and a goal, and then let them work on developing it freely until a set due date. Make sure they have scheduled time to work on the project, build content, and step away so they can return with fresh eyes. Give them necessary resources, as well. Examples of what you'd like to see, whether from other businesses or internal efforts that can be improved upon, are a great start.

Most importantly, step away once the project is assigned, and don't ask to see it until the due date. If you hover or continually check in, your supervision can stifle creativity, or set an unspoken expectation that ideas remain within certain boundaries. You don't want doers, ready to obey when it comes to connected messaging. You want independent thinkers who aren't simply at work to put in their time and fly below the radar. If you don't give space to think independently, it won't happen.

Allow uninterrupted presentation. Whether your team member(s) provide a write-up, a campaign idea, or an actual in-person presentation with a slideshow, allow them to share their ideas without being interrupted or shot down before they've finished. Stay open minded, take note of areas where you have relevant knowledge or information, and gauge the project's creativity and alignment with vision and brand.

Allowing for uninterrupted idea development, and then uninterrupted presentation, sets the stage for success. This way, you can get an accurate idea of what your team members are capable of when given time, resources, and direction, and left to make the most of it. This also benefits business owners. You save time by letting ideas grow without constantly checking in, saving that work for after the presentation.

Assess results and adjust accordingly. Letting go of micromanagement is the hard part. If your entire process simply consists of idea development, presentation, and then complete acceptance/rejection of the idea, you are unfortunately creating doers simply trying to get approved, not thinkers willing to take risks.

Instead, at this stage, a conversation needs to happen. What parts of the idea are realistic? What needs better alignment to reach goals? Is this person (and any teammates) still the ideal team member for the task?

At this point, you learn pretty quickly who the creative problem-solvers are, and that alone is worth the time and resources invested so far. For those who may not be a good fit for this task, there is surely another one for which they are, and this project may have helped reveal it.

There is often still a little more work to be done at this stage, but at least now, a foundation of mutual respect and investment has been laid. You want your business to succeed, and your team members want their idea to succeed. Work together to reach those goals, and you'll find campaigns more enjoyable and effective the further you take them.

It can be tempting to make things easier by putting on rose-colored glasses and creating seemingly simple processes. Processes make everyone look equally capable, when really there are probably team members who spend all day struggling to meet process milestones, and others who hit them well before lunch. The latter likely have much more they can bring to the table, but again, they must be given the time, space, resources, and direction to do so.

Learning what your team is capable of is a huge part of connection, and connection is how you reach new customers and retain existing ones. Your team needs the freedom to grow. Outdated team management dampens your marketing and kills your business. You need to have a connected, creative, growing internal team in today's business world to thrive.

Appreciation, Not Acquisition

Dr. Jones was born and raised in the small east coast community where he runs his practice, and it shows in the best way. Everyone seems to know him. They also know his daughter, whom Dr. Jones wanted to bring into the business a couple years ago.

The practice would need more patients to expand to two providers. Dr. Jones already had one thing going for him: warm and fuzzy reviews dominated his online presence. His four-member team didn't just know patients by name, but by their personal stories as well. No one was simply a patient number.

The team really cared about the people they served, and it showed.

Their retention was great, but acquisition needed a boost in order to form a father-daughter team. Recognizing that he already had a strong community presence, Dr. Jones began increasing his digital presence, using stock photos and promotions to create social media posts and ads to attract new patients.

When it didn't get as big a response as he'd hoped for, he called me for help.

After looking over the practice's marketing assets, I found a company to work on updating the practice's website and digital brand. Then, I made an unexpected request.

"Can you dedicate some of your time to community outreach and patient appreciation?"

Dr. Jones was surprised. He was already quite well-known in the community, and his high retention showed that patients were clearly satisfied! I didn't back down, however, asking if he could commit to setting time aside each month to call, text, and even write letters to local businesses and charities he could collaborate with, and to patients just to say thank you. Dr. Jones obliged.

Together, Dr. Jones and I reached out and worked with pet shelters, schools, and other organizations to hold community and customer appreciation events. Meanwhile, I boosted the practice's internal marketing to highlight a tool possibly even stronger than reviews: referrals.

*It seemed like a lot of work, putting all this effort into connecting with already loyal patients. But, in just six months, the number of new patients walking through the door had **nearly doubled**.*

What happened? Before, patients kept coming back to the practice they could trust. Now, with more engagement and community connection, people outside of the practice took notice as well. What's more, the photos, videos, and stories produced by the engagement all provided more fuel. The best content was used on Dr. Jones' various social media pages.

These events and personalized outreach efforts hardly felt like marketing on either end of the conversations, and that's the point. Dr. Jones' appreciation campaign was so successful, he had to scale his efforts back to accommodate his busy schedule.

The interesting thing about this story is that the practice already had the great online reviews businesses typically struggle to attain. Even highly successful businesses have a hard time with this if their client base isn't active on review sites.

This strength alone, however, was not enough. Dr. Jones needed to show up for his patients outside of the office if he wanted more than he already had from them. He needed to connect more deeply. Once he showed that he cared about patients even when they didn't have an appointment, everything else fell into place.

The most valuable thing you can give someone is time, especially in this digital age.

I've mentioned this problem before. Many business owners get so obsessed with their acquisition number, that they lose sight of other important factors that would better help their business grow. Earlier, I talked about how this quantity tunnel vision can prevent a business from getting quality customers. Now, I'll talk about how focusing on appreciating current customers can boost your bottom line.

Your best (and most affordable) source of new customers is your current customer base. Word of mouth and referrals are still alive and well in the digital age.

How do you get current customers to bring you new customers? Be engaging. Be appreciative. Be something worth sharing.

Appreciation Messaging

Reaching out from a place of appreciation doesn't have to be difficult. In fact, you probably already do it in your personal life quite easily.

Here are a couple of simple situations where appreciation messaging works well in business:

> **Customer Milestones.** One great way to create engagement is by celebrating customer milestones. A milestone can be a birthday, graduation, first-time experience with your business, or an anniversary of doing business with you.
>
> The week of a milestone, surprise your customers. Send them a card, flowers, baked goods, or an appropriate or quirky gift. Imagine the experience customers will have, and the great things they will have to say to their family and friends about your business's kindness.
>
> If the customer reaches out to say thank you, tell them they're welcome! If you're feeling brave, ask if they'll take a picture and post it to social media, tagging your business. You'd be surprised how far

happy customers are willing to go for you, and this effort on their part boosts your online presence and your best referral source, word of mouth.

Use these moments to create your own special moment with your patient by building these connections.

Holidays. Holidays are a great time to get engaging. Contests, campaigns, and decorations can really leverage festive feelings.

A great example is Halloween. Halloween candy can be a parent's worst nightmare, but it doesn't have to be. Initiate a Candy Buyback program, and reach out to your customers to let them know. Allow children to bring or send in their Halloween candy and earn money based on pounds or pieces. Done right, this is a great way to advocate for healthy eating and financial literacy, and build engagement while appeasing parents and children alike.

For bonus points, ask customers to fill out a quick survey about your business's strengths and areas for improvement at the end of their holiday experience, and measure these results. Offering a small raffle prize can help incentivize this. You'll get quick feedback about your business to help identify what you're doing well, and how you can grow.

Thanksgiving, for another example, is a great time for a food drive. Let your customers know that your business is collecting canned goods and other items for the holidays. You might be surprised by how many donations you'll receive, all of which can go to a local charity.

Create Engagement With Customers

People, by nature, want to make a difference even if it is one canned food at a time. Create engagement with your customers and build your reputation simultaneously. Remember, the more positive an experience they have with your business, the more likely they are to come back and bring friends and family along.

In-office engagement is also crucial for any successful business. It promotes a friendly and energetic workplace culture and makes the atmosphere better for team members and customers alike.

When team members are happy, customers feel better about their choice to do business with you. Your team's positive interactions with customers doesn't just help with retention. They boost word-of-mouth recommendations, too.

While identifying your ideal target audience is essential, it's also important not to forget about people once they convert from audience to customer. Your returning customers already believe in you, trust in you, and keep coming back to you. They also know other people like themselves. If you aren't giving existing customers a platform to tell their friends about you, you're losing out on your number one referral source.

Social media and online review sites are the big word-of-mouth platforms today, which is why it's so important to have a presence there. How do you stay present online? By engaging with people offline, then sharing it to these platforms.

Let's take an extreme example. A small, brand-new business has just opened. Every single customer is new, but hopefully will return. Since that is the goal, a lot of energy is put into making sure every customer has an amazing experience, and a chance to spread the word about that experience to their friends. Maybe there's a gift, or raffle for checking into the business's location on social media, or for posting a picture with a product.

These are great ideas, but we can take it further.

Appreciate every customer you gain, but also extend appreciation to the community you're in, the organizations you work with to keep your business open, and the people who make it happen, especially your team. Reach out to the local Y, the library, farmer's market, schools, and the chamber of commerce to find out how you can best show your appreciation for the community. If you offer a service like healthcare, for example, consider opening your doors from 4 p.m. - 7 p.m. twice a year to provide complementary health screenings to the community.

You want people to trust you, like you, and feel able to have a conversation with you. If someone doesn't know who you are, allowing them to experience a soft touch with your business through a pop-up, tabling, or community outreach event can help break that barrier to new customers.

Social Media Translation

Facebook is modeled after the real world. Users are connected to friends, fans, coworkers, family members, college professors, and more. Users can private message one another, just like a private conversation in the real world, but what they post on their timeline or in a review is quite different.

Posting to a Facebook timeline or business page is like talking loudly at a party where your Facebook connections are in attendance. Not everyone will hear what is said, but many will, or can, if they chose to enter the same room.

What are your customers saying to the room about your business? Did you make them smile? Feel cared for? When people at that party hear about your customers' good experiences, they'll be more likely to turn to you for those experiences themselves. This is possibly your most accessible, affordable acquisition tool, and all you have to do is be present and engaged on social media to activate it.

Why spend a majority of your time and money attracting a cold market, an audience that may or may not be looking for what you offer? By giving your existing, happy customers a platform within their social networks of people in similar demographics, you access a much warmer audience.

Now, here's the important thing. This whole chapter is about appreciation, right? Don't forget that. Follow through with appreciation all the way to the end. *Thank your customers for talking about you.* This is one of the biggest mistakes I see business owners make. They go through all this effort to create a good impression, connect with customers, ask for reviews, and be present on review platforms so it can happen. They send emails and texts, make calls, and set up a team script to ask for reviews. After all that effort, when they finally get a positive review or a shoutout, what do they do?

Nothing.

It doesn't make sense. If someone walked into your business and said an existing customer referred them, wouldn't you contact that existing customer to say thank you, or at least thank them the next time you saw them? Saying thank you is the human thing to do. It's how we strengthen connection.

At the end of the day, your customers are going to talk about you. As your strongest referral base, it's smart, and good business, to give them good things to talk about. Show your appreciation for them in the best way you can, and they'll spread the word to family, friends, digital and social media, and beyond, breaking through marketing white noise with the power of human connection.

Reputation, Not Chatter

Michelle has been in business for thirty-four years. As an international speaker and coach, she's known for being knowledgeable, friendly, and direct. She's a straight-to-the-point, no-fluff kind of woman, with a smile.

Michelle has this wonderful ability to help people see the best in themselves. She doesn't preach, acting as if she knows more or has more experience than her audience. Instead, she works alongside her listeners, seeking ways for them to improve themselves together.

Despite her people-focused approach to life and work, however, Michelle's marketing content told a different story. Touting her accomplishments, expertise, and talent, her messaging looked, well, a lot like everybody else's.

This wasn't an accurate reflection of Michelle and her approach. When she was ready to expand her business, she knew something had to change. It was hard to pinpoint what to change, however. She'd been providing the same quality for decades, and her audience admired the ways in which she helped them. She sensed that there was a lot of white noise she was competing with, but how could she break through?

She gave me a call, and after I took a look at her messaging, I told her something she might not have been ready to hear.

"Michelle, you're going to have to get more personal."

Michelle needed to share stories that illustrated the camaraderie she offered her audiences. All of her "talented, experienced expert" messaging wasn't helping people relate to her. Her decades of success were based on connecting with people on a personal level, not on the success itself.

For a straight shooter like Michelle, it was tough at first to offer as much vulnerability as her audience offered her. We started by sharing short stories that illustrated how people benefited from her help, rather than posting her own success stats. These stories quickly got more social media reactions than previous posts.

We shifted her messaging away from her and began to focus on her clients. People responded, seeing themselves in the stories of people who had found new levels of success. I encouraged Michelle to double down on this engagement, to respond to every comment, even just by liking them. She quickly found that replying to comments started conversations, which was the kind of engagement she needed to make a personal connection.

Meanwhile, for clients in her seminars, we made it easier for attendees to leave feedback as they wrapped up their experience. The reviews started flowing in. We used them as content for more success stories and watched engagement and seminar registrations grow. Her social media followers more than doubled in just a couple of months.

By refocusing her messaging onto the people she wanted to help, rather than on how great she was at helping, Michelle gained more followers and more clients.

We're all great at what we do; at least we think so! That's why we do it, and why we've built a business around it.

But guess what? Everybody else in business feels that way, too. The messaging centered around being good at what we do is everywhere. It's so noisy that it becomes chatter, something many of my clients have struggled to overcome by the time they reach out to me.

While it can be tempting to join in on the chatter (after all, you're also pretty experienced and talented!), you must resist the urge. Chatter doesn't stick. It's like the unengaging posts that look like all the others on a social media feed. People scroll past, looking for something that they connect with. To make that connection, your business has to be more than good. It has to be *known* and *respected* by people in your audience's network. You need a great reputation, and that comes from customers, not you.

There are certainly things you can do to shape your reputation. Having a strong business name, well-designed logo, and colors that align with the impression you want to set are all a good start. At the end of the day, however, your brand isn't really these things. It's what customers say about you when you are not present. It's word of mouth.

In my years as a marketing strategist, one thing I've realized is that as soon as a business moves away from self-focused chatter and shifts focus to their audience, everything changes.

Your reputation is how you make someone feel. Someone other than you has to say, *This business is amazing!* Ideally, they say it where other people can hear or see it.

What makes people say a business is amazing? It's when they feel a connection. That is how you build reputation.

The Reputation Pyramid

I like to envision reputation-building as a pyramid with four levels. The bottom of the pyramid (**Gain**) forms a foundation, and each level above that (**Provide, Manage, and Share**) builds upon the foundation until the pyramid is complete. I'd like to share my Reputation Pyramid with you. Hopefully it helps you envision your own business's reputational success.

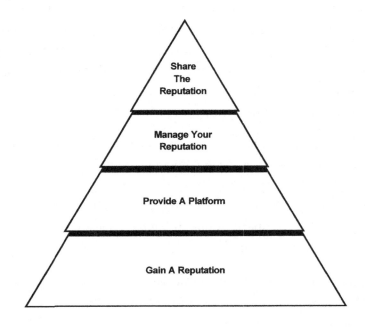

Foundation: Gain A Reputation

Your brand is what people say about you. It's not about you, but them, and your messaging should reflect that. Get people talking about your business, and you're on the way to a strong reputation.

Consider customer service. What is your business's approach to working with people who come to you for help? What is their first interaction with your business like? How are phone calls answered? All of these situations are (hopefully) handled in a way that puts the customer experience first. You ask, *How would my customers like to be treated?* and respond accordingly. Your messaging should do this, too.

Successful businesses center the customer in their messaging. If you are trying to attract young families, for example, think like them. Dinnertime can be hectic. Perhaps you can make their lives easier with a meal delivery service. Or maybe they'd appreciate movie tickets for the whole family or some other family-friendly experience.

I'll tell you what they don't want: another branded mug. They probably already have a cabinet full of those kitchen versions of brand chatter. Mugs are fun and easy, but dig a little deeper and you'll find much more meaningful results. That family will remember the fun or delicious experience you provided. You break through the chatter by focusing on things that actually benefit your target audience.

This is important for existing customers, as well. Know their birthdays and anniversaries and do something special. Emails are a start. I certainly enjoy all the birthday emails

I get from various businesses I work with. But if you have the time, and an in-house marketing ambassador, send personalized, signed birthday cards. Going beyond sending an automated email shows that you're actually thinking about your customers on their special day.

Second Level: Provide A Platform

Many businesses have great reputations because they're good at what they do. That's why they're in business. It's not enough to simply gain a good reputation, however. You also need to provide a way for that reputation to be shared with the world. Customers need a place to talk about you so that you can harness that super effective word of mouth!

There are plenty of digital review sites serving this exact purpose, but you can also do it internally. A coffee shop, for example, might have a corkboard, paper, and pens with a sign inviting people to pin up their feedback as they leave. If placed strategically, this can be visible to others walking by.

As for digital platforms, many businesses send reminders to customers, asking them to write online reviews. One thing I've noticed, however, is that asking via text, email, or social media posts is not enough. Much more effective are in-person requests for a review, especially as a response to someone saying they had a great experience.

Letting people know that they can expect a text or email with a review link increases the chances that they'll actually read the message and follow through, rather than just see it as more chatter or spam to be ignored. Use human interactions to make the connection to your digital presence, and customers will see leaving a review as a way of returning the favor for great customer service.

Not everyone is savvy enough to go online and find you on their own. Once you have a platform, tell customers what it is, and make it easy for them to find it. Be mindful of the fact that not every customer has an account on a review site, so tailor review invitations to those who do.

With a strong customer connection, and by providing the tools to let customers share their experiences, your business begins to build a reputation and a presence that shares that reputation with the world.

Third Level: Manage Your Reputation

We established that you need to thank your customers for good reviews. That's a small step towards managing your reputation. The bigger, harder step is properly handling the negative ones.

Some businesses only reply to negative reviews. This is not good reputation management. When I say management, I mean that you have to reply to *all of your reviews*. That's your reputation. Your reputation online is like the one you have in person. If someone did something nice to you in person, you would say thank you. If someone reaches out for a handshake, you offer your hand in return.

Replying to all reviews, including the good ones, has three benefits:

1. The people who wrote your review see your reply and are reassured that you really do care. You took the time to actually read the review and thanked them. They will likely continue to talk positively about you, building your reputation.

2. Replies are more online content. The web crawlers and algorithms looking for active businesses will see engagement, your back and forth conversations, and an active online presence. This helps with your business's online search result ranking.

3. Potential customers who see this will realize that you care about all reviews, positive and negative. I don't know about you, but I want to spend money at a company that cares about customers. Seeing your replies to every review, good and bad, reassures a potential customer that if they have a bad experience, you'll listen and try to make it right.

A quick note on negative reviews: fake reviews happen, and the approach to handling those is different. Not every review is written by an actual customer, so context is important when constructing a response. Still, you don't want to leave these negative reviews hanging around, fake or not.

Managing your online reviews benefits you in so many ways, and isn't all that different from non-digital feedback. If somebody sent you a handwritten card, thanking your business for great service, you would call them back and thank them. Treat people online as you would treat them in person.

Pro tip: Make a note in a customer's file when they write a review. Next time you see them, bring it up. Thank them in person, make a big deal about it, and reference what they said. If your team knows that a customer wrote a review, and shows appreciation, the customer will likely become one of your best advocates.

Top Of The Pyramid: Share That Reputation

At this point you have a reputation, and people are talking about it on platforms you've provided. You reinforce your reputation by responding to reviews. Now, you need to broadcast all of this work so that others can see your potential. The moment you stop sharing, you stop utilizing the power of your reputation.

This takes more than automating reviews to pop up in a feed, or sharing every review using the same format every time. Those methods simply become chatter. Sharing must be personalized.

At the same time, you can't broadcast a look-how-great-we-are message. Remember how that held Michelle back? You still, even at this stage, have to make it all about the customers. Your messaging has to be, *Here's why we do what we do for you,* or, *Here's the feedback we get from customers, and this is why we do this work.*

The information has to be about them. You can be vulnerable here, sharing how reviews make you feel. *When we receive this feedback, it makes our day. Thank you for trusting us with your needs and choosing us. We appreciate you.*

You can share this gratitude in multiple ways. Include a photo or video of the team saying thank you as content on your social media. Get creative with your thank you's, using a fun GIF or a photo of a customer with a big smile. Focus on the satisfied customer, especially in your caption and text, allowing potential new customers to see themselves in those shoes.

Chatter Is White Noise

In our digitally savvy world, word of mouth no longer just means in-person conversations. Digital platforms allow customers to share their opinions with thousands, if not millions of people across the globe. More than ever, consumers can make or break a business, making marketing methods evermore arbitrary.

There's no reason to fear, however. You know that you're great at what you do, and your customers likely know this, too. This means you have a huge source of strong, positive messaging already interacting with your business. All you need to do is activate this source so that they can spread the word.

Provide a platform, manage responses, and share reviews to rise above the white noise and chatter. Start with doing what you do best—meeting your customers' needs—and let that connection fuel your journey beyond outdated marketing tactics.

Niche, Not Broad

Jan is an athlete and educator who is passionate about helping her audiences achieve work-life balance and avoid burnout.

As someone who changed careers after experiencing burnout herself, Jan relates to her listeners. She cares about her work, keeping up to date on the latest findings so she can pass the information on to those who turn to her for help. Her goal is to change people's lives for the better.

Jan had a personal social media presence, but not a business one. She kept hearing about how important being on social media was for a business, but she wasn't sure how to leverage it. There were so many platforms, and it was overwhelming to imagine managing so many pages.

"You need videos! Graphics! Hashtags! Ads! Targeted ads! Chatbots! Funnels!" her colleagues kept insisting. Unsure of where to start, she began spending money on social media management solutions. When it didn't seem to work, Jan called me.

After meeting with Jan, I explained that if she wanted to use social media, she had to approach it just like any other marketing. Start by identifying who she wanted to get in front of.

Of course, this didn't mean Jan needed to upload entire presentations to social media to attract her target audience. That wouldn't be good for business! What we needed to do was use social media to position her as a thought leader. Social media is more than funny memes; it's a tool that allows you to get in front of large audiences based on your content. It's especially effective for establishing your business within a niche.

We decided to create a social media calendar to organize her efforts. We made a plan. This went beyond looking up cute holidays like Chocolate Ice Cream Day and posting a picture of her team enjoying ice cream (though that was certainly fun). We focused the calendar template on the audience, and asked ourselves, What can we post that will benefit the audience, and demonstrate that Jan is a thought leader in her field?

For example, when she was scheduled to discuss burnout in an upcoming speaking engagement, we planned a short Facebook Live video session for her to tease the topic and answer some viewer questions in real-time. The next day, she would share a relevant article. She'd continue sharing something new all the way up until her speaking engagement.

When Jan and I first began creating the calendar, she had some hesitation. It was a big time commitment, for one thing, but Jan had also never done a Live video before. As with anything new, it can be intimidating to put oneself out there. What if there was negative feedback? What if something went wrong and couldn't be undone? Compared to her usual well-rehearsed talks, a Live video was a less controlled environment. It felt risky.

I reframed the calendar and Live session so that Jan could see the benefits. Anyone in her network who had a question about burnout would begin to see her as someone to whom they could turn. As an expert in her field, creating content and being available to answer questions was her best draw for potential new business. What's more, Live videos were right within her wheelhouse as a speaker.

We moved forward, filling our content calendar. We centered it around the question, How do we support clients with content? Once we created the calendar and began following it, Jan's social media engagement started growing.

Today, Jan is getting attendees for her speaking engagements, clients, and direct networking opportunities with other industry thought leaders thanks to social media. Previously, her social media engagement was zero. Now, after customizing her content, social media is one of her top sources of conversion.

In Jan's case, this approach worked because she was personally a part of the content creation. Likewise, if you are the face of your brand, you have to be actively participating in and sharing the content. Even in my own Facebook group, engagement drops when I travel and I'm not personally posting. My team members post on my pages to keep them active while I'm away, but engagement from followers still drops without me there.

In addition to personal investment in your messaging, I'm going to reiterate a previous idea: vulnerability is important. Every time I have shared a story about a time I made a mistake or had a learning experience, I've seen a bump in feedback and engagement.

People appreciate genuine business owners. They want to know that we are people, too.

Social media can seem intimidating, with so many people operating impersonally from behind a screen. But sharing vulnerability and the not-so-pretty parts of your business journey along with successes shows people your authenticity. Honesty in content is like taking away the perfect lighting, makeup, and digital touch-ups of photos so common in mass media. That authenticity cuts right through the white noise of marketing that's killing businesses everywhere.

Here's Some Good News

When it comes to social media, many of my clients want to know if they need to be on *all* of the platforms.

My answer is, *absolutely not.*

You only need to be on the platforms where your target audience is. In Jan's case, based on her audience, she only needed to be on three platforms: Facebook, Instagram and LinkedIn. This was based on the age range and nature of Jan's field of expertise. A business focused more on current events may need to be on Twitter, businesses in the videography field will need to be on TikTok, and so on.

I meet many customers who believe they *have* to be on social media, and they do so without any real plan, strategy, or even idea of which platforms they should be on. The truth, however, is that the process for creating a social media campaign remains the same as any other. First, identify your target audience. Then, find the platform where they are, and define your goal. This might be brand awareness, direct conversions, or like Jan, establishing an image as a thought leader.

Then, figure out what kind of content and messaging you want to share based on your audience and goals. And, now that you've learned about leveraging content, you can make the most of it.

The audiences on these platforms are changing all the time, which does require a little ongoing work to make sure you're still targeting the right audience with your online presence. For example, seniors and baby boomers are a growing Facebook audience. Depending on your business, that may mean becoming more active on Facebook, or redirecting that energy elsewhere.

That being said, constant audience change is, in some cases, an understatement. By the time this book is published, boomers could be abandoning Facebook for something else. Sometimes, adding a new platform to your messaging repertoire offers insurance against these fluctuations.

Content Repurposing

If managing multiple social media platforms sounds overwhelming to you, you're not alone. But I'm going to let you in on a little secret.

It's way easier than you think.

Imagine a business that's done their homework: they've identified a target audience, defined their goal, and figured out what platforms best accomplish that goal for their audience. They've decided that they need to do a direct mail campaign, newspaper ad, and radio ad.

Two of those platforms are print, and the radio ad will be built from a script. Should the business assign three separate, isolated teams to create a unique ad for each platform, from start to finish, with no communication between teams?

No. That might be good for brainstorming or A/B testing a range of ideas, but a smart business will likely want the final versions to represent the business uniformly. While the creatives for each platform will be different, the messaging needs to be consistent. Consistency means potential customers are seeing the same messaging repeated on multiple platforms, whether through a radio jingle or eye-catching text. Repetition helps with memory retention, and when potential customers remember you, your conversion goes up.

The direct mail, newspaper ad, and radio ad will probably perform best if the language is at least similar across all three. The business's team will come up with the best language and repurpose that content across all platforms.

This is not a new strategy, but it can certainly be used in a new way with social media. Let's look at an example.

You make a Facebook Live video. Perhaps it's a Q&A, a product review, or an interview. All of these are strong choices depending on your goals, and video is a great medium given the state of internet content. A study by Cisco[2] in 2018 predicted that, by 2020, 82% of online traffic will be video. Video is certainly getting a lot of action, so making one is a great step.

Now, how can we leverage that content by repurposing it across multiple platforms? Let's explore the possibilities:

1. You can download your Live video directly from Facebook and, with a little reformatting, post it to Instagram for IGTV.

2. You can cut snippets out of the video for your Instagram story.

3. The video can go on your business's YouTube channel. With the right SEO strategy, it will show up when people search for related content.

4. You can embed the YouTube video on your website. This gets visitors watching your video without

[2] "Cisco Visual Networking Index: Forecasts and Trends, 2017-2022 White Paper," Cisco VNI, last updated February 27, 2019, https://www.cisco.com/c/en/us/solutions/collateral/service-provider/visual-networking-index-vni/white-paper-c11-741490.html.

affecting site speed, since an embedded video is not directly on the site.

5. The video can also be linked in your email campaign.

6. You can add the video to your blog, as part of a welcome page or post.

7. The video can be included in internal marketing for training, or in-office TV screen content.

8. Screenshots and snippets from the video can become photos for LinkedIn, Twitter, Facebook stories, website content, and more.

9. The video can be added to online profiles, such as your Google Business page, to directly appear in the search results.

10. It can also be shared with the press.

That single piece of content can be repurposed for at least ten different purposes. Leveraging content across all channels this way is a smart marketing move.

This content repurposing approach has many benefits:

1. It maximizes the use of each piece of content created.

2. It reaches different people and networks, opening up opportunities for new populations to connect with your business's messaging.

3. You can create more content from it.

To repurpose content well, of course, you need to be sure you are utilizing the various platforms correctly. Instagram requires proper sizing and hashtags, YouTube needs titles and tags, and the video needs to play well on mobile devices when sent through newsletter systems.

Don't post a video on every platform without doing your homework. Optimizing content is about more than just posting it. If you're not sure how to do it right, ask for help from someone who does.

Asking For Help

I've said it before, and I'll say it again. You need someone on your team committed to managing these campaigns to make them work. That being said, what should you look for in a social media manager?

You may have heard the quote by Peter Schutz, CEO of Porsche, "Hire character. Train skill." In my experience, this is true for all hiring, but especially true in the case of choosing a social media manager for your business.

You may be thinking, "But Minal, the social media manager needs to know how to work the platforms. Skill is important!"

Of course skill is important. But what sells on social media? Being social. You need someone in your business who is fun, creative, a quick learner, and most of all, an extrovert. This individual is going to be responsible for socializing with your customers, asking them to take photos and videos, running your social media campaigns, creating contests, engaging with comments and getting your team excited about it all.

Obviously, if you can find someone who is also familiar with social media platforms, that's great! If not, that's okay. Skills can be learned. Just as you go to conferences and take courses to advance your skills, so can your social media manager. It's exactly how I got my start.

The important thing is to have content that is shareable and interactive. Focus on getting someone who can do that, and the rest will follow.

With so many social media platforms competing for attention, it's easy to feel overwhelmed. It's also easy to see why audiences are too overwhelmed by marketing to connect with the businesses they need. This makes it even more important to approach social media with intention. Jumping into the fray without a plan is wasted energy. Take time to go through all the steps you would with any other campaign, repurpose your content, and have a dedicated team member. Your social media presence will see much more return for your effort.

When you do things just to do them, they're meaningless. When you do things with intention, that's when you really get somewhere. Connecting to your niche, rather than casting a broad net, is a big game-changer when it comes to conversion.

Don't Market, Connect

When I started my first company in my twenties, I certainly had some fears. After all, I was young and relatively new to the field. I wondered whether I would be taken seriously and whether my passion would be recognized and supported.

Like many of us, I wanted my entrance into the business world to make a big splash. It was also important to me to do something meaningful. Launch parties were the trend at the time, but I was determined to break through the noise and connect with my audience in a way that stayed true to my vision and values.

My team and I began to narrow down ideas about how we could launch in a way that helped the community. Secretly, I had a desire to break a Guinness World Record. When I finally blurted the idea out, I immediately dismissed it as an idea that was too out there. My team, however, was having none of it. With a go-getter attitude that still makes me smile today, my team of millennial women got to work.

October, Breast Cancer Awareness Month, was coming up. We personally knew families affected by breast cancer who cared about raising awareness. As a dental hygienist and marketing strategist, my team and I also wanted to bring awareness to Dental Hygiene Month, which was also in October. I wanted to highlight the connection between oral health and overall health.

After much strategizing and connecting, the Swish Away Breast Cancer event was born. We leveraged our various skill sets, marketing strategies, and community connections, including one with the local Old Bridge High School football team. We planned a half-time show where we invited the community to be a part of something truly special: breaking a Guinness World Record for using mouthwash while bringing awareness to both breast cancer and dental hygiene.

A total of 1,530 attendees showed up to swish mouthwash at the same time, all wearing bright pink shirts complemented by the pink uniforms of the football team's cheerleaders. We connected with breast cancer survivors and researchers to inform them of the event, with the goal of spreading awareness about breast cancer and oral health in a fun way. We had one banner with my company name, but otherwise didn't mention my business or draw attention to it.

The point of the event wasn't my business; it was doing something good for the community. We focused on connecting with people, which aligned with my business goals. As a happy byproduct, I now had dozens of community connections interested in my skill set.

By shifting focus from marketing my company to connecting with the audience, we broke the record for the most amount of people swishing mouthwash at the same time, brought awareness to important issues, participated in multiple interviews, and had fun. This event was covered on TV and by the local and national press. I was asked to interview for podcasts and news channels and was contacted by influencers for features. The launch was a complete success.

"Your marketing is killing your business" is a bold statement, coming from a marketing strategist. But I stand by it, and hope that after reading this book, you agree. Our current marketplace is ad heavy. The number of marketing platforms and methods available to businesses is overwhelming. Customers are fatigued. It's tough to break through the noise.

As businesses fight for attention, they understandably highlight their best qualities. But if everything is shiny, then nothing is shiny. Everything becomes one large, blinding message that's difficult to look at, let alone process.

For example, maybe your business's highlight reel is powerful, but next to everyone else's powerful reel, it loses its effect.

We see everyone around us using these tools, and feel we need to jump in and start using them as well. We build websites, create social media presences, and start sending email blasts to our mailing lists. We join the fray, not wanting to be left behind, and get frustrated when our beautiful website has few visits, our social media platforms have no engagement, and our email blasts have low open and click rates.

What are we doing wrong? We're doing what everyone else is doing, and it must work for them, so why isn't it working for us?

The problem is that we take these forward steps without really knowing why we're taking them. In the process, we may even wind up distancing ourselves from our customers instead of attracting them. At best, we're not reaching our ideal customers. At worst, our attempts at fitting in come across as ingenuine.

Customers can sense a lack of understanding and be turned off by the appearance of a business not truly being with the times, or of trying too hard.

Doing the same thing as everyone else adds to the noise. Doing it without connecting with the audience makes it unproductive. As a marketing strategy, not connecting simply doesn't convert—and isn't conversion the point?

Marketing that doesn't convert isn't marketing. Without conversion, your marketing is killing your business one dollar at a time.

* * *

Now that you've read about some of my favorite strategies for connecting, think about your current marketing campaigns, and ask yourself:

- Why are you doing the marketing you're doing?

- Who are you trying to attract to your business?

- Do you need all of your marketing? Is it all converting?

Think about the companies you do business with, and the

companies you frequent as a consumer yourself. What drew you to those companies? Was it their mission? Their quality? Perhaps you know someone at the company that you trust?

Most likely, you chose those companies because in some way, you connect with them. Something about the way they do business, or the people conducting the business, aligns with your values and beliefs. Many businesses sell products and services, what makes you choose one specific company?

You may have seen some of their advertising, but ultimately, you committed because of a connection. Your customers do the same with you.

So many people see technology as the complete solution. They'll fire off an email campaign, expecting the leads to come rolling in. When nothing happens, they're frustrated. All that time, effort, and money spent for no return on investment. Why didn't it work? Doesn't everyone use email? Yes, everyone does use email. And that's a problem. To stand out with email, you need great subjects, content, and/or a well-established connection with your audience. Successful email campaigns are very intentional in their effort to connect, or leverage connection.

We can't keep attempting to bank on the outdated idea that the coolest, hippest new marketing tool is all we need to stand out. Technology ages just like anything else. Internet search is thirty years old, and email is forty. Fatigued consumers scroll past paid ads at the top of search results pages and delete a spam email without even opening it.

These methods are not marketing solutions. They are tools. If you want to build a house, you don't pick up a hammer and start nailing boards together. First, you make a plan, a blueprint.

Your blueprint has to include what message you are trying to convey, what you are trying to accomplish, and who your message is for. Only with this plan can you decide whether you need a hammer, a mallet, a screwdriver, or a contractor who knows a lot more than you do about how to get the job done.

Without a plan, marketing is pointless. What is the point of promoting products and services to the wrong audience, on the wrong outlet, and/or without a message that connects with customers despite all the noise?

Use marketing as a tool to connect, rather than a means to a sale's end. Talk to people rather than just inundate eyeballs. Connection will get you where you want to go.

The Future Of Connection

My husband and I recently restored a 1969 convertible VW Beetle. It took over eighteen months for the car to take a trip fifty years back in time.

When I first saw the restored car, I was taken aback by the simplicity of the design. It's small: two doors, skinny seats, no dashboard, tiny glove compartment, no armrest, no cup holders, and you have to manually open the windows.

At first, I noticed all the things that were missing, especially compared to my SUV with keyless entry and other luxuries. But the brilliant thing about simplicity is that it removes the excess, connects you with the goal, and makes you appreciate what you have. When you really think about it, how many of your car's features do you actually need?

When my husband and I took it out for a spin, the Beetle did exactly what it was made to do. It took us from one destination to another. After a couple of drives, we didn't even miss the extra features anymore. We had everything we needed to get from point A to point B. The features in our more modern vehicles were nice but didn't necessarily contribute to the ultimate goal.

Just as with cars, technology and platforms will progress, changing the ways in which we live and communicate. Business owners will find success by cutting the fluff, focusing on finding and connecting with customers over commonalities. Actively connecting with people means giving them an opportunity to reach out. It means identifying which outlets best support that connection for your business. It means being approachable, and providing helpful information, especially in our information-heavy age.

Showing up for your customers in this way builds a relationship that will outshine the marketing white noise and propel your growth despite constantly changing technology and markets.

Getting new customers and keeping the ones you've got is no longer about standing out. Rather, it's about standing with customers, helping them reach their destination without unnecessary knickknacks and doodads. Don't just be present. Be active.

What Can We Expect To See In The Near Future?

As I write this, in 2019, social media sites are encouraging more activity in groups on their platforms. They prompt interaction by making it easy for people to ask and answer questions, ask for recommendations, and more. This infusion and respect of human knowledge and experience in digital spaces is a great representation of what our future will look like.

Technology will continue to make it possible to reach

audiences faster than ever imagined. And while it's important to stay with the times and keep up with the technology, it's also important to remember why the technology exists. It exists to connect. We are trying to reach humans, not machines. People want to be cared about, feel special, be heard, and know that they matter to you and your business.

This is why scandals have such huge repercussions for businesses today. Alienate certain audiences with insensitive practices or messaging, and a business can lose a huge part of their customer base. People don't want to work with businesses they don't feel respected by, but they absolutely want to work with those they feel understand them and want to make a difference.

Review sites mean that consumers now hold the microphone when it comes to business feedback. It also means that they can expose poor practices or questionable owner decisions. Just look at the number of actors and politicians today who are out of a job due to poor personal decision making. Consumers and people in a business owner's network can voice their opinion loudly, clearly, and globally. If someone feels wronged, everyone will quickly know, and decide whether they want to continue to support that person or business accordingly.

On the other hand, consumers also have the power to broadcast what is great about you and your business. Put customers first, contribute to communities and causes your business believes in, and watch the results unfold. If you can make your customers feel heard and respected on an individual level, they can share that connection globally, and build your messaging for you. Through reviews, conversations, and more, your customers can become your best marketing channel.

Connecting In 2025

Five years from now, I expect we will see more convergence of convenience and direct authentic communication.

Consumers today demand convenience, and businesses are responding. Amazon has grocery stores without checkout counters, scanning items via camera as shoppers pick them up, and charging their account as they walk out the door. Rideshare apps allow riders to quickly summon door-to-door transportation and track their driver's whereabouts and ETA. In a few years, if it isn't easy to communicate with you, your business will feel the effects.

Accomplishing this means going beyond your product or service. It means being a person, being authentic, and using technology to let others access you.

We talked about creating a customer avatar. Something I think businesses will need to do moving forward is to create a *business avatar*. Who is your business? Who wants to be friends with it? How does your business meet new friends? Your business is a living entity and has a personality of its own. It has likes/dislikes, things it'll stand for, and things it won't.

In this book, we discuss many ways your business can make new friends or customers. These methods open up opportunities for your business avatar to connect with your ideal customers in a meaningful way. When people see your business personality for what it is, whether through a manifesto, the causes it supports, or the way it treats customers, that connection converts.

By building meaningful relationships and leveraging evolving technology, you'll never have to market again: simply connect.

Acknowledgments

Writing my first book has been both challenging and exhilarating, and I couldn't have done it alone. This book is the product of many people's guidance, support, and talents. My deepest gratitude goes to my childhood friend turned esteemed writer, Shannon Burton. Thank you for transforming our countless conversations, tangents and all, into these pages. They became the map to our journey, and I would not have reached this destination without you.

Henry, you motivated me to be an author. Thank you, truly. To Parul Agrawal, you made the most daunting task easy. Thank you for delivering this book to the world. I also must recognize my incredible team; each and every one of you is a true champion. Thank you for sharing your talents with me.

My heartfelt thank you to the colleagues, friends, and mentors who have helped me throughout this process. Your time and efforts made the complexities of book writing manageable. Whether brainstorming title ideas or teasing out important details in early drafts, your contributions have not gone unnoticed. Thank you for your generosity and honest feedback.

Mom and Dad, I can never thank you enough for giving up your comfort so that I could fulfill my dreams. So much of who I am today, I owe to you. To Arjun, Bijal, Reeva, Penny, and the rest of my family: thank you for being my biggest cheerleaders. And of course, to my husband, Andrew, thank you for being my constant.